Ma

SEPT

Beaton
Callum
Lewis
MacCaig
MacLure
Malcolmson
MacAskill
MacCorkindale
MacNicol
Nicholson
Norman

MacLeod

MOTTO:
Hold Fast

CREST:
A Black Bull's Head with Gold Horns
between two Red Flags with Black Staves

PLANT BADGE:
Juniper

TERRITORY:
Skye, Harris, Lewis, Soay,
Raasay, Assynt, Gairloch

MacLeod

by Hamish McLeod

Lang**Syne**

PUBLISHING

WRITING *to* REMEMBER

LangSyne
PUBLISHING
WRITING *to* REMEMBER

Vineyard Business Centre,
Pathhead, Midlothian EH37 5XP
Tel: 01875 321 203 Fax: 01875 321 233
E-mail: info@lang-syne.co.uk
www.langsyneshop.co.uk

Design by Dorothy Meikle
Printed by Ricoh Print Scotland
© Lang Syne Publishers Ltd 2009

ISBN 978-1-85217-076-9

Chapter one:

The origins of the clan system

by Rennie McOwan

The original Scottish clans of the Highlands and the great families of the Lowlands and Borders were gatherings of families, relatives, allies and neighbours for mutual protection against rivals or invaders.

Scotland experienced invasion from the Vikings, the Romans and English armies from the south. The Norman invasion of what is now England also had an influence on land-holding in Scotland. Some of these invaders stayed on and in time became 'Scottish'.

The word clan derives from the Gaelic language term 'clann', meaning children, and it was first used many centuries ago as communities were formed around tribal lands in glens and mountain fastnesses.

The format of clans changed over the centuries, but at its best the chief and his family held the land on behalf of all, like trustees, and the ordinary clansmen and women believed they had a blood relationship with the founder of their clan.

There were two way duties and obligations. An inadequate chief could be deposed and replaced by someone of greater ability.

Clan people had an immense pride in race. Their relationship with the chief was like adult children to a father and they had a real dignity.

The concept of clanship is very old and a more feudal notion of authority gradually crept in.

Pictland, for instance, was divided into seven principalities ruled by feudal leaders who were the strongest and most charismatic leaders of their particular groups.

By the sixth century the 'British' kingdoms of Strathclyde, Lothian and Celtic Dalriada (Argyll) had emerged and Scotland, as one nation, began to take shape in the time of King Kenneth MacAlpin.

Some chiefs claimed descent from

ancient kings which may not have been accurate in every case.

By the twelfth and thirteenth centuries the clans and families were more strongly brought under the central control of Scottish monarchs.

Lands were awarded and administered more and more under royal favour, yet the power of the area clan chiefs was still very great.

The long wars to ensure Scotland's independence against the expansionist ideas of English monarchs extended the influence of some clans and reduced the lands of others.

Those who supported Scotland's greatest king, Robert the Bruce, were awarded the territories of the families who had opposed his claim to the Scottish throne.

In the Scottish Borders country - the notorious Debatable Lands - the great families built up a ferocious reputation for providing warlike men accustomed to raiding into England and occasionally fighting one another.

Chiefs had the power to dispense justice

and to confiscate lands and clan warfare produced a society where martial virtues - courage, hardiness, tenacity - were greatly admired.

Gradually the relationship between the clans and the Crown became strained as Scottish monarchs became more orientated to life in the Lowlands and, on occasion, towards England.

The Highland clans spoke a different language, Gaelic, whereas the language of Lowland Scotland and the court was Scots and in more modern times, English.

Highlanders dressed differently, had different customs, and their wild mountain land sometimes seemed almost foreign to people living in the Lowlands.

It must be emphasised that Gaelic culture was very rich and story-telling, poetry, piping, the clarsach (harp) and other music all flourished and were greatly respected.

Highland culture was different from other parts of Scotland but it was not inferior or less sophisticated.

Central Government, whether in London

or Edinburgh, sometimes saw the Gaelic clans as a challenge to their authority and some sent expeditions into the Highlands and west to crush the power of the Lords of the Isles.

Nevertheless, when the eighteenth century Jacobite Risings came along the cause of the Stuarts was mainly supported by Highland clans.

The word Jacobite comes from the Latin for James - Jacobus. The Jacobites wanted to restore the exiled Stuarts to the throne of Britain.

The monarchies of Scotland and England became one in 1603 when King James VI of Scotland (1st of England) gained the English throne after Queen Elizabeth died.

The Union of Parliaments of Scotland and England, the Treaty of Union, took place in 1707.

Some Highland clans, of course, and Lowland families opposed the Jacobites and supported the incoming Hanoverians.

After the Jacobite cause finally went down at Culloden in 1746 a kind of ethnic cleansing took place. The power of the chiefs was curtailed. Tartan and the pipes were banned in law.

Many emigrated, some because they wanted to, some because they were evicted by force. In addition, many Highlanders left for the cities of the south to seek work.

Many of the clan lands became home to sheep and deer shooting estates.

But the warlike traditions of the clans and the great Lowland and Border families lived on, with their descendants fighting bravely for freedom in two world wars.

Remember the men from whence you came, says the Gaelic proverb, and to that could be added the role of many heroic women.

The spirit of the clan, of having roots, whether Highland or Lowland, means much to thousands of people.

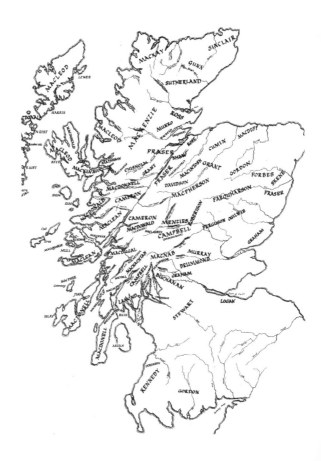

Chapter two:

Rulers of the Hebrides

From the end of the eighth century the west of Scotland was subjected to a barrage of attacks by Vikings and Norsemen who came from Norway to settle in the Shetlands. They used the northern isles as a base for their plundering and by the end of the 12th century their descendants, the Kings of Man, a mix of Celts and Norsemen, also ruled the Hebrides.

According to Clan tradition MacLeod is believed to be descended from a Viking ancestor, Leod, who was the son of Olaf the Black, King of Man and the Northern Isles. Leod, who lived in the 13th century, was a very powerful chieftain. When the King of Norway gave up the Hebrides to the King of Scots, Leod took advantage of the confusion that followed to extend his territories to cover most of Skye, a sizeable part of Lewis and Harris, and parts of the mainland including Appin.

It is said that Leod acquired Dunvegan

Castle on the Isle of Skye when he married the heiress of the Norse family who owned much of the land on Skye, early in the 13th century. Leod died around 1280, and in accordance with the Scandinavian traditions of the time, his lands were divided between his two sons, Siol Tormod and the Siol Torquil. Tormod, who appears to have been the elder, was given a bigger share of the lands of Skye, Harris and in Glenelg. The lesser lands were allocated to Torquil and it was this division which spawned the two distinctive branches of the clan – the MacLeods of Harris, Glen Elg and Dunvegan; and the MacLeods of Lewis and Assynt.

The Gaelic names are Clan Tormod (Thormoid) and Clann Torquil (Thorcuil). Little is known about the MacLeods or their chiefs around this time. Few local records survived and the men from whom these chiefs held their lands were the important figures in national terms.

In an attempt to increase their sway in the remote northern territories, the King of Scots gave away a lot of land to influential noblemen who

became the superiors over local communities and in the case of the MacLeods much of their land was given to the Earl of Ross.

During the wars of independence in the late 13th and early 14th centuries, the Earls of Ross variously sided with fellow Scots and enemy English. The MacLeods themselves remained loyal to their country and Tormod was one of Robert the Bruce's leading supporters, fighting alongside him at Bannockburn.

In 1357 John of Islay, having by marriage united the claims of several families, declared

himself Lord of the Isles. The same family later
gained the earldom of Ross, becoming the feudal
superior of almost all the Hebrides, including the
lands of both branches of MacLeods.

These Lords of the Isles were laws unto
themselves and paid little heed to the King of
Scots. The history of the island clans in the 14th
and 15th centuries is very much taken up with the
fortunes of the Lord of the Isles. One of them,
Donald, led a force of Highlanders and islanders
in 1411 and seized Inverness before crossing the
Spey to grab more land and march right to
Aberdeen. But they were intercepted by the fighting men of the northeast, under the command of
the Earl of Mar at Harlaw, two miles north west of
Inverurie. A bloody conflict ensued which nobody
really won. All the surviving MacLeods and other
clansmen could do was lick their wounds and
make their way home. This was a battle which
epitomised the conflict between the Lowlands and
Highlands of Scotland as the Lord of the Isles
attempted to expand his lands at a time when the
monarchy was weak.

Chapter three:

Hold Fast!

**In the fourteenth century Malcolm MacLeod
of Glen Elg was said to be in love with Fraser
of Glen Elg's wife and when he was returning
home from a secret meeting he was met and
confronted by a savage bull.**

He killed it, reputedly by breaking its
neck, and in the struggle one of its horns broke
off. The horn was late made into a drinking cup
tipped with silver and became known as the drinking cup of Rory Mor, after a famous MacLeod
chief. When the MacLeod chief comes of age he
is expected to drain it.

Long ago one of the MacLeod chiefs
of Dunvegan went to Inverary to visit the Earl
of Argyll and when he was there he was invited
to attend the execution of a Campbell who had
misbehaved and who was to be gored to death
by a bull.

When the man was led into the arena he

showed such calm courage that the MacLeod
pleaded for his release but Argyll declared this
would not be possible.

MacLeod asked if he could jump into the
pit and save the man thus securing his release.
Argyll reluctantly agreed but added, 'You go to
your death.' MacLeod leaped down and as the
bull lowered its head for the charge he seized one
of the horns and clung on as he was tossed about.

A spectator shouted, 'Hold fast!'

He did so and managed to stab the bull with his dirk. It is said this is why the bull's head and the motto, 'Hold Fast' are in the armorial bearings of the MacLeods of Harris to this day.

The bull's head crest was built into the wall of St Clement's Church at Rodil in Harris by Alasdair Crottach, 8th Chief of MacLeod, early in the sixteenth century. He died while building was in progress and a horizontal string course of black layered rock diverted around the bull's head was incorporated in the design – it is a traditional mourning band of the MacLeods.

Historically, black bulls were an ancient symbol of royalty and often symbolised the death of an enemy chief. Ancient Egyptians used to kill bulls and, using chants, would 'transfer' their sins into the head of the bull thus absolving themselves of any wrong doing.

A black bull's head was set before the young chief of the Douglas clan during dinner at Edinburgh Castle in 1440 in an episode which became infamous in history as The Black Dinner. Shortly afterwards he was executed.

Chapter four:

The Fairy Flag

Dunvegan Castle on Skye has been occupied by the same family for the last seven centuries, making it the oldest continually inhabited house in Britain.

The ancient walls, home to more than 20 generations of MacLeod chiefs, rise from the summit of a rocky crag above a sea-loch. Water surrounds three sides of the castle and on the landward side it is protected by a fosse which is sixty feet wide but no longer as deep as it was in the Middle Ages. Until 200 years ago the only way into the castle was by the Sea Gate, where steep stairs led up the side of the rock. Now a bridge affords entry.

Dr I. F. Grant, the famous historian, had this to say about Dunvegan: 'Throughout the history of the MacLeods there runs a thread of tenacity that worthily fulfils their motto, Hold Fast. In nothing is this staunchness better shown that in the maintenance of the bonds uniting the chief and his clansmen.

'In no other clan have such ties been so consistently maintained. Samuel Johnson and Boswell described how they had survived the break-up of Highland society following the '45. Archives show how faithfully the chiefs continue to fulfil their obligations.

'Doctors were maintained, in the fine tradition of the old Lordship of the Isles, education was fostered and heavy expenditure incurred in road-making. MacLeod's private post to Edinburgh was for long a boon to the community. Grain was imported in times of scarcity. Agricultural improvements kept pace with the most enlightened in the country.'

If you visit Dunvegan you can see the Brattich Shithe, the famous Fairy flag, which is more than a thousand years old and measures four feet by two. It came through the Norwegian ancestry of the family and was possibly a saint's shirt kept to bear in peace of war as a lucky relic.

But a clan legend says a faery princess

married a MacLeod and as she was summoned back to fairyland she dropped her cloak and that is the flag. Another tale says that when a MacLeod heir was born his nurse slipped away to watch or take part in the carousings. The bedclothes slipped off the new baby and faeries wrapped him in a silken flag. When the nurse returned she carried the baby into the great hall and mysterious voices said the flag had magic powers.

If produced in battle the flag would ensure victory and make an enemy believe that the MacLeods had more men than they actually had. At one time when the MacLeods were out-numbered by the Clanranalds they produced the flag and the MacLeods were multiplied tenfold in the eyes of the Clanranalds.

The flag was carried into battle rolled up by its hereditary keepers as the MacLeods believed it should only be unfurled in times of danger such as when plague threatened the community. By looking after it well the flag would ensure the succession of the family, according to popular belief, and would bring herring into the loch, which meant prosperity. But it could only be waved three times and if a fourth were ever to take place the flag would disappear from the earth.

In 1799 an estate factor forced open the iron chest holding the flag while the chief was away and it is believed his foolhardy action led to the fulfilling of a prophecy by the Brahan Seer – the chief's heir was killed at sea in a ship explosion.

Chapter five:

Massacre and revenge

Feuds were a constant feature of clan life in the 16th century. The Crown could not keep order and its policy of using some clans to try and control others caused a lot of trouble and resentment. The MacDonalds and MacLeods were constantly fighting each other and the Frasers were another foe.

One of the most shameful and bloody episodes occurred after a MacLeod, in retaliation for an atrocity carried out against some of his men, attacked the island of Eigg, a MacDonald stronghold. There he found the whole population hiding in a cave. He ordered fires to be lit at the cave mouth and the smoke suffocated all inside.

The MacDonalds then hit back by sending huge numbers of their men to Skye. They landed near Dunvegan where many MacLeods were attending a church service. The church was set alight and the congregation burned to death except one woman who managed to escape and informed her chief of the atrocity.

He at once prepared to march on his enemy but seeing them approach the castle in vast numbers MacLeod retreated to Dunvegan and summoned the fairy flag. This was waved at the MacDonalds who immediately fell under the spell of imagining they were vastly outnumbered. They turned to flee and many were killed trying to reach their boats.

During the 16th century the MacLeods were also torn apart by internal divisions about the chieftanship. When William, the ninth chief, died in 1552 his only child, Mary, succeeded to the title. But a cousin claimed he was the rightful heir.

In the ensuing power struggle several innocent people were murdered and for a time, the clan was ruled by a dictator. But he was driven out by the late chief's younger brother, Tormod, who became the clan leader. Tormod also resolved the problem over Mary's inheritance by arranging a marriage for her and gave her the MacLeod land. Thus the chieftanship of the clan and the lands themselves were reunited.

In the same period several disputes began in the Lewis branch of the clan which lasted for 50 years and ended in the ruin of that family. Rory, son of the 10th chief of the Lewis MacLeods, married a Mackenzie but then claimed the first son she bore was not his. Consequently Rory disinherited the child.

Mackenzie of course supported his grandson who pressed for his inheritance for many years after his death. Much blood was spilled and in the process the local population was reduced to poverty.

Chapter six:

Courage and blood

In 1596 the Government demanded that all the Highland chiefs should show their title deeds of land to prove ownership. The chief of Lewis failed to provide the necessary documentation and so had his lands forfeited. These were handed over to a group of Lowland gentlemen known as the Fife Adventurers.

The idea was that these men would colonise the island and make local industries such as fishing profitable. Under the scheme a share of the profits would be returned to the Government.

Not surprisingly this met with stiff opposition and after much fighting the Adventurers were forced to quit and went home.

In 1608 the experiment was tried again, without success, but the fighting of 50 years had so weakened the islands that when Lord Mackenzie launched a further assault in 1610 they were unable to resist.

The MacLeod leader, Neil, held out until a large number of the women and children of the island were threatened with drowning and he was forced to surrender. Later Neil was executed in Edinburgh and Lewis was lost to the Mackenzies.

The chief's family was exterminated by Mackenzie and it was then represented only by cadet branches. The main line of the Lewis MacLeods, the descendants from Leod, had disappeared largely as a result of internal feuding within the family.

Rory Mor, chief of the Dunvegan MacLeods, also failed to produce his deeds in 1596 and his lands were forfeited. However they were returned to him by crown charter of 1611, at which time he seems to have found real favour with the king.

He was a clever man, apparently the first MacLeod chief who learned to write, and was shrewd enough to adopt the right attitude to the more strongly enforced rule of central Government. In time this strict rule was to decline and the finances of the family, which had suffered greatly in the 16th century, grew stronger.

Rory encouraged interest in the finer things of life such as piping and poetry. From his own household came Mary MacLeod who instigated some new techniques which led to a great flowering of Gaelic poetry in the 17th century.

In the 1640s, twenty years after Rory's death, the wars of the Convenanters began. In the early years MacLeods took little active part though they supported the Covenanters in principle.

However after the execution of Charles I in 1649 events had gone too far and the MacLeods did not support the new regime, distinguishing themselves in battles fought in the 1650s.

In 1650 Charles the Second was asked to come to Scotland and an army was raised to try and regain the throne but it was soundly defeated in the battle of Dunbar.

Another army was then formed consisting mainly of Highlanders, including a strong contingent of MacLeods. It was led personally by King Charles and met Cromwell's highly trained army at Worcester in 1651. There a great battle was fought. The MacLeods were in the main body of Highlanders who fought with courage and tenacity but they were hopelessly outnumbered. Eventually the strength that comes with greater numbers prevailed and the Highlanders were pushed back to Worcester which had earlier been badly damaged by canon fire. Around 3000 were killed, many in battle and others as they attempted to escape. Around 700 of the casualties were MacLeods.

Brave efforts by the Scots to resist Cromwell's invasion failed and the MacLeods, like most clans, had to make peace with the new Government – peace bought with a large sum of money.

The MacLeods had suffered badly in the cause of Charles II but they got no thanks from the King when he eventually did regain the throne. Enraged by this ingratitude Roderick the chief swore that the MacLeods would never again fight for the Stewart king.

Consequently MacLeods took little part in

the Jacobite rebellions of the 18th century. The MacCrimmons, the most famous family of Scottish pipers, are septs of the MacLeods and for centuries were hereditary pipers to the chiefs. They had a college at Borevaig on Skye.

John Dubh MacCrimmon, last of his race to hold the hereditary post, decided to emigrate to America in 1795. He must have been a very reluctant migrant because when he reached his port of embarkation at Greenock his love for his own land overcame him and he returned to Skye.

Many Highlanders, including MacLeods, went on to distinguish themselves in regiments. The chief of MacLeods took his men off to fight in the American wars of independence, just one of the many conflicts in which clansmen distinguished themselves with bravery and determination. On his return from America he formed the second battalion of the Black Watch in 1780 and his proud boast was that most of his men carried the surname MacLeod.